History and Activities of
Ancient Egypt

Alexandra Fix

Heinemann Library
Chicago, Illinois

© 2007 Heinemann Library
a division of Reed Elsevier Inc.
Chicago, Illinois

Customer Service 888-454-2279
Visit our website at www.heinemannlibrary.com

Designed by Kimberly R. Miracle in collaboration with Cavedweller Studio
Originated by Chroma Graphics
Printed in China by WKT Company Limited

11 10 09 08 07
10 9 8 7 6 5 4 3 2 1

The Library of Congress has cataloged the first edition as follows:
Fix, Alexandra, 1950-
        History and activities of ancient Egypt / Alexandra Mary Fix.-- 1st ed.
                p. cm. -- (Hands-on ancient history)
        Includes bibliographical references and index.
        ISBN 1-4034-7923-2 (HC) -- ISBN 1-4034-7931-3 (PB)
        1. Egypt--Social life and customs--To 332 B.C.--Juvenile literature.
        I. Title.   II. Series.

DT61.F56 2006
932--dc22   2005035305
13-digit ISBNs:
978-1-4034-7923-5 (hardcover)
978-1-4034-7931-0 (paperback)

Acknowledgments
The author and publishers are grateful to the following for permission to reproduce photographs: Ancient Art and Architecture Collection, p. **12** (R. Sheridan); Bridgeman Art Library, pp. **18** (Egyptian National Museum, Cairo, Egypt, Giraudon), **22** (Louvre, Paris, France); Corbis, pp. **4** (Roger Wood), **7** (Archivo Iconografico, S.A.), **9** (North Carolina Museum of Art), **10** (Burstein Collection), **11** (Bettmann), **8**, **13** (Sandro Vannini), **14, 26** (Gianni Dagli Orti), **15** (Werner Forman), **16** (Archivo Iconografico, S.A); Harcourt, pp. **17** (David Rigg), **21** (David Rigg), **25** (David Rigg), **29** (David Rigg).

Cover photographs of a painting of an Egyptian king and queen (foreground) reproduced with permission of Alamy Images/Worldwide Picture Library and the Sphinx (background) reproduced with permission of Getty Images/Photodisc.

The publishers would like to thank Emily Teeter and Eric Utech for their assistance in the preparation of this book.

Table of Contents

Some words are shown in bold, **like this.** You can find out what they mean by looking in the glossary.

Chapter 1: Egypt, the Land of the Nile

The Nile River flows through Egypt. More than 7,000 years ago people farmed along its banks. They built homes on higher ground nearby. There were settlements in the north, called Lower Egypt, and in the south, called Upper Egypt. These regions were united around 3000 B.C.E. Their first pharaoh was King Menes, also known as King Narmer. Egyptian life centered around this **fertile** Nile valley. But the valley made up only ten percent of the country. A hot, dry desert covered the rest of the land.

The Nile valley was called the "Black Land" because of its dark soil. The desert was called the "Red Land" because of the sun's reflection on the hot sands.

Timeline

Egyptians use hieroglyphs.
3000 B.C.E.

Assyrians control Egypt.
671 B.C.E.

People settle near the Nile.
5500 B.C.E.

Egypt unites and first pharaoh rules.
3000 B.C.E.

First pyramid is built.
2700 B.C.E.

Persians rule Egypt.
525 B.C.E

Flooding and farming

Every year in July, the Nile River overflowed its banks. The waters flooded the surrounding land for four months. By November, flooding stopped and the ground began to dry out. The waters left behind sticky, black mud that was good for growing crops. Next came the planting season. Farmers used oxen to plow the fields. They scattered seeds by hand while the ground was still wet. In May the crops were gathered and stored. By July flooding began again. It was important that the river flooded each year. Without the rich soil left behind, crops would not grow well. The people might starve.

Greeks conquer Egypt.
332 B.C.E.

Romans conquer Egypt. **30** B.C.E.

Cleopatra VII is the last Egyptian queen.
51 B.C.E.

About dates

The phrases B.C. and B.C.E. show that something happened before Jesus was born. The phrases C.E. and A.D. show that something happened after Jesus was born. On this timeline you can see that Rome conquered Egypt 30 years before Jesus was born. With modern dates we do not usually use C.E. or A.D. Everyone assumes we are talking about today.

The gifts of the Nile

The Nile is the longest river in the world. It is about 4,145 miles (6,671 kilometers) long. Its main source is Lake Victoria in modern-day Uganda. The Nile flows north through Egypt and empties into the Mediterranean Sea.

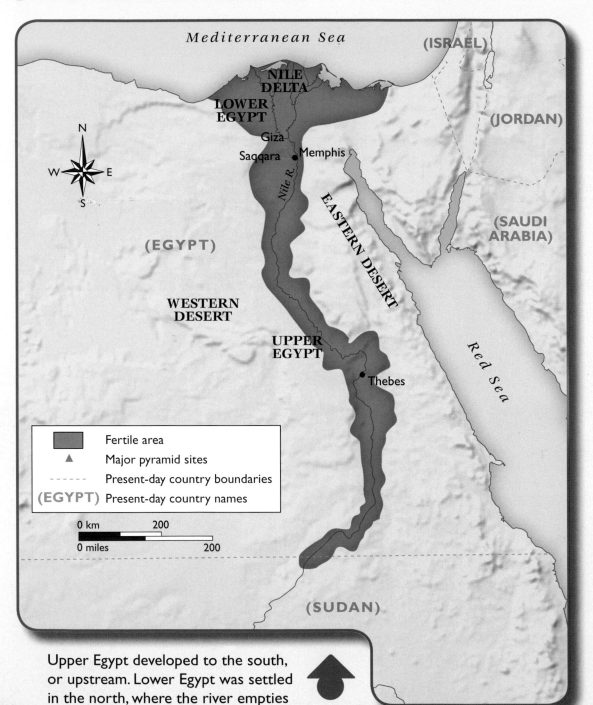

Upper Egypt developed to the south, or upstream. Lower Egypt was settled in the north, where the river empties into the Mediterranean Sea.

The ancient Egyptians lived and worked along the banks of the river. They also lived along streams that branched out from the Nile. The river gave them water for drinking, bathing, and watering crops. The river kept the soil **fertile**. Crops grew well. There were fish, birds, and other animals nearby for food.

The river also helped in other ways. River mud could be formed into bricks to build homes. A plant, called flax, grew along the Nile. Flax could be woven into cloth. The river was also a source of **papyrus**. Papyrus was a type of river reed. It could be made into paper, rope, linen, sandals, baskets, mats, boats, and rafts. The Nile provided all that was needed. Egypt became a strong, independent nation.

Egyptian rulers

Powerful kings, called pharaohs, governed Egypt. People believed that the pharaohs were like gods. Most pharaohs were men, but not all. Queen Hatshepsut ruled for 21 years. She dressed like male pharaohs. Tutankhamun became king at the age of nine. He died when he was only eighteen.

Until 1000 B.C.E., rule by pharaohs was strong. After that, Egyptians were controlled by the Assyrians and Persians. Later, Alexander the Great conquered Egypt for Greece. After Alexander's death, one of his generals became king. Cleopatra VII was a **descendant** of that general. She became the last queen of Egypt. Egypt was defeated in 30 B.C.E. It became part of the Roman Empire.

This gold funeral mask was found in the tomb of Tutankhamun in 1922. Historians believe that this is what the boy-king looked like.

Egyptian writing

Egyptians were some of the first people to have a written language. They used a type of writing called **hieroglyphics**. Symbols and pictures stood for objects and sounds. Later, the symbols became simpler. They looked more like cursive writing. These later styles were called hieratic and demotic.

Sometimes hieroglyphs were carved into the walls of tombs and temples. Sometimes they were written on **papyrus** with a brush and ink. Papyrus pages could be pasted together to form a scroll. Egyptians wrote down records of important events. They also recorded everyday life. Because the people wrote so much down, we know many details of Egyptian life.

The Rosetta Stone was discovered in 1799. This stone had the same story written in three languages. It was written in hieroglyphs, demotic, and Greek. The Greek words helped scholars to translate the Egyptian words. The Rosetta Stone helped scholars understand the meaning of the hieroglyphs.

The Step Pyramid at Saqqara was designed by Imhotep, the first architect whose name was ever recorded.

Pyramid tombs

The Egyptians built tombs and monuments of stone. These buildings honored the pharaohs. The Step Pyramid at Saqqara was one of the earliest stone buildings ever made. Egyptian workers built it without using cranes, pulleys, or wheels!

Growing and gathering

There was not much rain, so Egyptians had to **irrigate** their crops. They dug **canals** to bring water closer to the fields. They also invented a machine called the *shaduf*. A bucket was put into the water. A lever with a weight on the end lifted the full bucket to water the fields. Irrigation is still important in Egypt today.

The Egyptians knew many things about growing and gathering plants. They also kept bees and collected honey. Honey was used for food and medicine.

Egyptians were the first people to make ships with wooden planks almost 5,000 years ago. They used wood from Syria and Lebanon. Their basic ship design is still used today around the world.

Family life was important to ancient Egyptians. Young girls helped their mothers in the home. Boys learned to work with their fathers. Girls and boys married in their teens. Families were big, and some had 15 children. Most Egyptians died by their mid-30s.

Husbands and wives were equal, but they had different roles in the family. Women cooked and cleaned. They cared for the family and made clothing. They also made things to trade. Women could have jobs outside the home. They could be weavers, servants, bakers, musicians, and dancers. They could also own and sell property.

In ancient Egypt, parents, children, grandparents, and other relatives often lived together in the same home.

There were more than 2,000 gods and goddesses in ancient Egypt. Each one was in charge of a different part of life or death. Ancient Egyptians worshiped in private and in public. Prayers and **sacrifices** were offered to the gods.

More than 50 pyramid tombs were built in ancient Egypt.

Duty work

When a pharaoh began a building project, thousands of workers were needed. Peasants had to work a certain number of hours each year for the pharaoh. This was called duty work. Most duty work was done during flood season. Farmers could not work in the fields when they were flooded.

Social classes

A man's work decided his place in society. That did not usually change. Sons were expected to do the same work as their fathers. Education and military service were the only ways to move up. Most Egyptians were **peasants.** They worked as farmers, fishermen, and servants. Skilled craftspersons, soldiers, and merchants had more status. Scribes, priests, doctors, and engineers were very important people. The pharaoh was the most important. Slaves had the lowest social status.

Egyptian food, clothing, and shelter

Bread was the most basic part of an Egyptian meal. It was made from a type of wheat and barley. A drink was made from fermented barley. A typical meal might be bread, an onion or other vegetable or fruit, and a barley drink. Meat was not eaten often. But when it was it was usually fish, duck, or wild bird.

Peasants wore linen cloths tied around the waist and simple shirts. The upper class wore white linen robes. Sandals were made of papyrus. Men and women had different hairstyles. For special occasions, they wore wigs made of human hair. Children wore a sidelock. Both men and women wore bracelets, necklaces, and beaded collars. They also used an eye makeup, called kohl, around their eyes.

This clay model of a family's home is called a soul house. It would have been put in a person's tomb.

We have learned many things about the life and customs of the ancient Egyptians from scenes like this, painted on the inside walls of pyramids and tombs.

Ordinary Egyptian homes were made of mud brick. They were small and simple. There was an entryway, living room, sleeping room, and storage space. Most were only one story high. Meals were cooked in an outdoor courtyard or on the roof. There were low tables and woven mats for seats. Beds were often simple mats.

Getting around in Egypt

Egyptians walked almost everywhere. They used rafts or boats on the river for longer distances. There were no other vehicles ordinarily used. There was a carrying-chair used for officials and the queen or the pharaoh. Chariots were used only for military or hunting expeditions.

Boys and girls of ancient Egypt enjoyed running, jumping, and playing ball games. Children played leap frog, tug-of-war, and hopscotch. Boys played with marbles and wooden spinning tops. Girls loved dolls and dressed them in simple doll clothes. Board games, especially Snake and Senet, were popular among children and adults.

Egyptians swam in the Nile. They hunted wild animals and birds for sport. Another popular sport was wrestling.

The Serpent game was played on this spiral circuit with marbles and pieces in the form of lions.

Entertainment

Many Egyptians enjoyed music and dance. Most entertainers were women. Some of the favorite instruments were pipes, flutes, harps, tambourines, drums, and cymbals. Men and women did not usually dance together. Egyptians also liked to tell stories about their history and gods.

Wealthy Egyptians often enjoyed fancy parties with lots of things to eat and drink. Men and women wore their finest clothes to these parties.

This female lute player might be entertaining at a banquet or public festival.

More than a pet

The Egyptian Mau cat was tamed from an African wild cat. Modern housecats are **descendents** of the cats of ancient Egypt. Cats were kept as pets, but they also had important jobs. They killed poisonous snakes from the river. They kept rats and mice away from stored grain. Egyptians loved cats so much that they created and honored a cat goddess. She was named Bastet.

By doing the hands-on activities and crafts in this chapter, you'll get a feel for what life was like for people who lived and worked in ancient Egypt.

Recipe: Tiger Nut Sweets

Tiger Nut Sweets was a popular dessert served at a feast or celebration. This is one of the oldest recorded recipes. The original recipe was actually found written on a broken piece of Egyptian pottery, called *ostraca*. Papyrus was expensive, but *ostraca* was like scrap paper.

Ingredients:

- 12 dried dates, pits removed
- ½ cup walnut pieces
- ½ cup honey
- ½ tsp. cinnamon
- ½ cup ground almonds
(if you have a nut allergy you can substitute crushed cereal, graham crackers, or vanilla wafers for the walnuts and almonds).

Dates grow on one type of palm tree. Dates, figs, and pomegranates were fruits that grew well in the hot Egyptian climate.

1. Pour honey in a small bowl and mix in ground cinnamon.

2. Place ground almonds in another small bowl.

3. Stuff each date with walnut pieces.

4. Dip each stuffed date in the cinnamon honey to coat, then roll completely in ground almonds.

5. Serve at room temperature. Refrigerate leftovers.

Tiger Nut Sweets

Tiger Nut Sweets are finger food. Instead of using silverware, ancient Egyptians simply picked up their food with their fingers.

Craft: Papyrus and Hieroglyphs

To make papyrus, the Egyptians picked papyrus reeds from the Nile. The outside was peeled away and the inside was cut into thin strips. Strips were lined up next to each other. A second layer of strips was placed crosswise. The wet papyrus was then covered with linen and pounded with rocks. The plant's natural juices made the layers stick together. Once the papyrus was dry, it could be used as papcr.

Supplies:

- White glue or a cellulose-based paste
- Bright tempera or acrylic paint and brushes, or oil-based pastels
- Brown paper grocery bag
- Large salad bowl or popcorn bowl
- Wax paper

Warning!

This project is messy. Protect your clothing and work surface.

Read all directions before beginning the project.

Papyrus was one of the earliest kinds of writing material.

❶ Lay or tape wax paper down so that your project will not stick to your work surface.

❷ Water down about half a small bottle of white glue with an equal amount of water in a bowl. If you are using paste, water the paste down by using twice as much water as is suggested in its mixing directions.

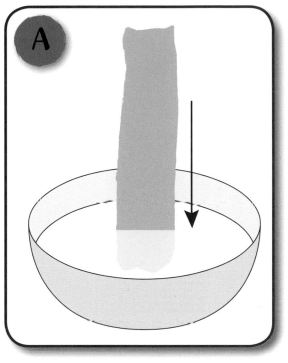

❸ Tear a brown paper bag into strips about two inches wide. Do not worry if the strips vary in width —ragged ends will bind together better than a clean cut.

❹ Dip one strip of the brown paper into the glue mixture. Make sure to soak it completely—and do not be afraid to get some on your hands! (See Picture A)

❺ When you take out the strip, slide it between your fingers to remove any extra glue mixture. Then place it horizontally on the wax paper.

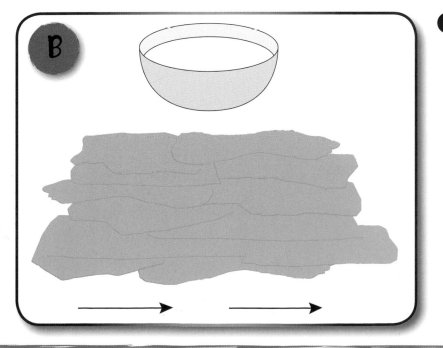

❻ Repeat this process, dipping another strip, squeezing out the excess, and placing the strip parallel to the first strip. The two strips should overlap a little bit along their edges. (See Picture B)

❼ Continue this process, placing more and more strips side-by-side until you have used about half of your brown paper. Press down on the strips to make the layer smooth. This is your first layer.

❽ To start making your second layer, use another strip, and dip and squeeze it like before. This time place it across the other strips, perpendicular to the first layer. (See Picture C)

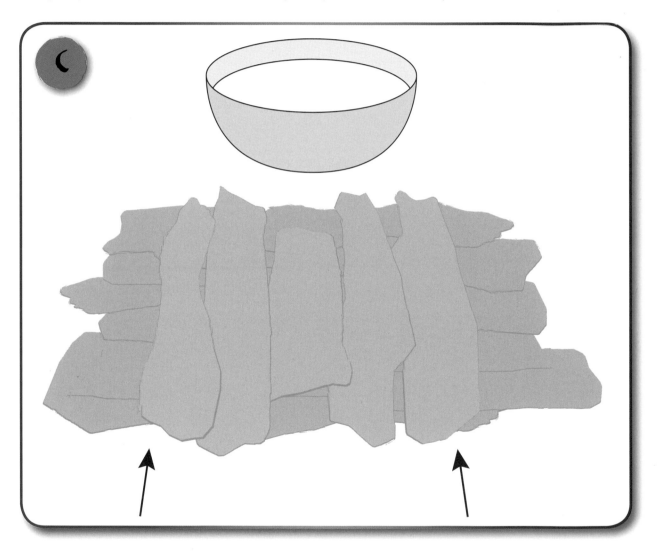

❾ Continue making more strips and placing them side-by-side on this new layer.

❿ When you have used all of your paper, press down on the strips to make the layers smooth.

11 Let the paper air dry overnight.

12 Once your paper is dry, you can use it. Use a pencil to create your design or message, then make it more permanent with the paints.

> What will you draw or write on your paper? How will what you write on this paper differ from what you would write on regular paper or on a computer? What might an Egyptian child write about?

Papyrus with Hieroglyphs

Hieroglyphic writing uses pictures, called hieroglyphs, instead of letters to record information or to tell a story.

Craft: Shabti Figurines

Egyptians believed that even after death the gods might require duty work, just like the pharaoh. Shabtis were figurines painted and buried with the dead. Egyptians believed that these magical statues could do someone's duty work in the **afterlife.** They would be brought to life by a spell when they wcre needed. The tombs of wealthy people sometimes held a shabti worker for each day of the year. Poorer tombs only had a few shabtis.

Warning!

Make sure to read all directions before beginning the project.

Supplies:

- Newspaper
- Masking tape
- Plaster gauze (available at craft stores) cut into about 20 one-inch by three-inch strips
- Markers

Each shabti was labeled with the dead person's name and a spell to bring the statue to life.

▶ Use newspaper to create an oblong, mummy-like shape. (See Picture A)

2 Wrap masking tape around the newspaper until the newspaper is completely covered, like a mummy. (See Picture B)

3 Dip strips of plaster gauze into water and use your fingers to remove the excess water. Cover the masking tape with the strips of wet plaster gauze, just like a mummy.

4 Decide what job you will give to your shabti.

What job would you most like your shabti to do for you?

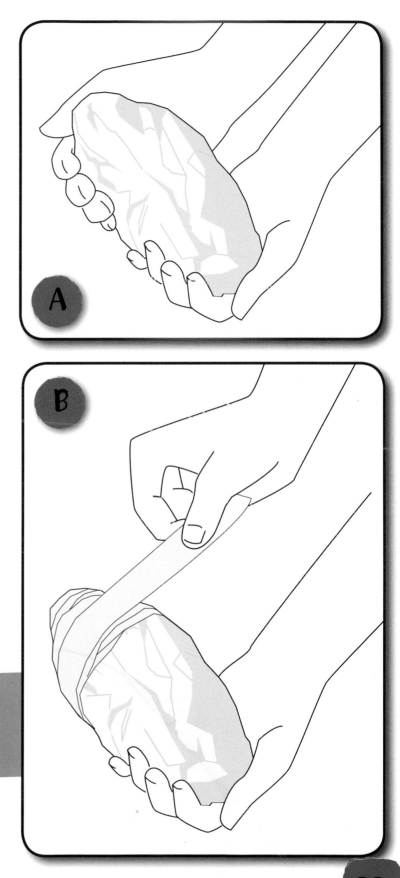

A

B

5 Decorate the face of the shabti in the Egyptian style. (See Picture C)

This shabti will clean my room in the afterlife. He will make the bed every day. He will pick up all of my clothes. He will make sure my books are on the shelf

6 Use markers to write on the gauze what jobs the shabti will do for you. Write as many details as you can so that your shabti will know exactly what to do. (See Picture D)

24

THIS SHABTI WILL CLEAN MY ROOM, MAKE MY BED, AND PICK UP ALL OF MY CLOTHES EVERY DAY.

Shabti Figurine

Your shabti figurine is made of a type of papier-mâché. Ancient Egyptian shabtis were made of stone, wood, pottery, bronze, wax, or glass.

What job would an ancient Egyptian child have chosen for his or her shabti?

Craft & Activity: Egyptian Senet Game

Senet was a popular Egyptian board game for children and adults. The name senet means "passing." Senet was played for fun, but it also had a deeper meaning. It might have been played as a symbol of the troubles a soul might have passing to the **afterlife.**

Four senet game boards were found in the tomb of Tutankhamun. One was trimmed with pieces of gold, ivory, and silver.

Supplies
- Posterboard or regular paper, at least three by ten inches. Or use the lid from a shoebox.
- Ruler
- Pencil or marker
- Checkers or similarly-sized counter or game pieces in two colors or shapes
- Dice or craft sticks

1. On the posterboard, paper, or inside of the shoebox lid, use a ruler and pencil or marker to draw a rectangle measuring three inches by ten inches.

2. Along a three-inch side of the rectangle, measure over one inch and make a mark. Without moving your ruler, measure over two inches and make another mark.

3. Repeat this process on the other three-inch side, measuring over one inch and two inches. (See Picture A)

4. Connect the one-inch marks from one side to the other. Do the same thing with the two-inch marks, so that you have created three columns, each an inch wide.

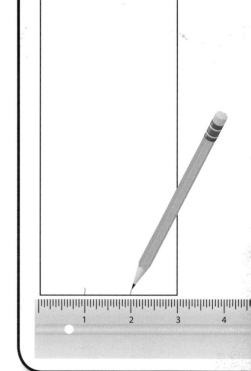

5. Use the same process to divide your columns into one-inch squares: Measure along one ten-inch line and make marks at every inch. Repeat this on a different ten-inch line, marking every inch. Connect the marks across all three columns. You should now have three columns of ten squares. (See Picture B)

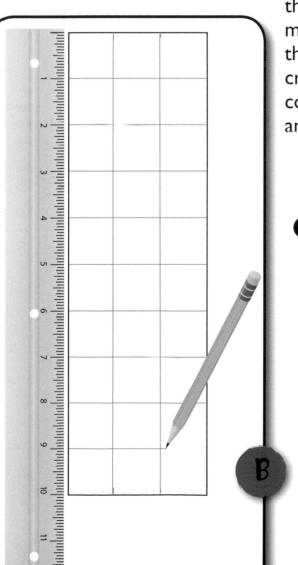

When you play this game, you will be moving your checkers or counter pieces around the board. To know how many spaces to move, you can roll a die. Or, to play a more authentic game, make throwing sticks to determine how many spaces to move. Draw an animal head on one side of a craft stick. Make a total of six craft sticks, each with a head on one side. Throw the sticks like rolling dice—the number of heads that land facing up tells you how many spaces you can move. (See Picture C)

How could you use more craft sticks or other materials for playing pieces? How could you make Egyptian-styled pieces?

How to Play Senent

Number of players: two

Goal: to be the first player to remove all counters off the board

1. Place the checkers in alternate colors down the left-hand side of the board. The players will move their counters up the left-hand column, down the center column, up the right-hand column, and then off the board. (See Picture D)

2. Throw the sticks or one die to see how far to move. Begin with the counter nearest to the start (the bottom left-hand corner of the board).

3. If you land on a square occupied by one of your own pieces, you can stay. If you land on your opponent's piece, you must go back to the start.

4. Players take turns.

5. When the first counter has passed the finish and is off the board, you start again with the second counter. Continue until all 5 counters are off the board.

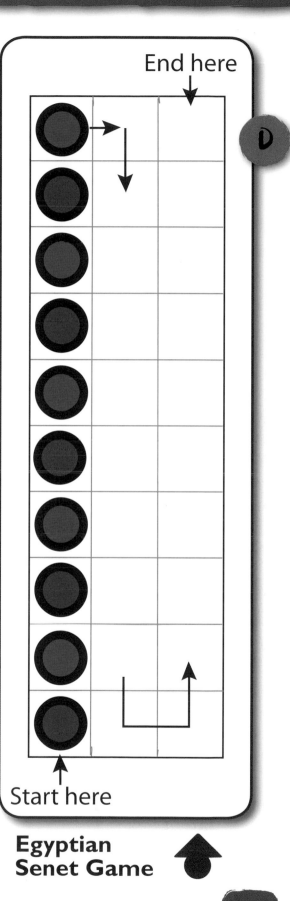

End here

D

Start here

Egyptian Senet Game

Glossary

afterlife life or existence after death

canal artificial waterway used for irrigation, drainage, or travel

descendant person or animal who comes later in a family

fertile good for growing

irrigate to water by means of ditches, canals, or pipes

peasant poor worker, often had to do the farm work for someone else who owns the land

More Books To Read

Armentrout, David and Patricia. *Egypt.* (*Timelines of Ancient Civilizations* series). Vero Beach: Rourke, 2004.

Chrisp, Peter. *Ancient Egypt Revealed.* New York: DK Publishing, 2002.

Hossell, Karen Price. *Hierogylphs.* (*Know It* series) Chicago: Heinemann Library, 2003.

The instructions for these projects are designed to allow students to work as independently as possible. However, it is always a good idea to make a prototype before assigning any project so that students can see how their own work will look when completed. Prior to introducing these projects, teachers should collect and prepare the materials and be ready for any modifications that may be necessary. Participating in the project-making process will help teachers understand the directions and be ready to assist students with difficult steps. Teachers might also choose to adapt or modify the projects to better suit the needs of an individual student or class. No one knows what levels of achievement students will reach better than their teacher.

While it is preferable for students to work as independently as possible, there is some flexibility in regards to project materials and tools. They can vary according to what is available. For instance, while standard white glue may be most familiar to students, there might be times when a teacher will choose to simplify a project by using a hot glue gun to fasten materials for students. Likewise, while a project may call for leather cord, it is feasible in most instances to substitute vinyl cord or even yarn or rope. In another instance, acrylic paint may be recommended because it adheres better to a material like felt or plastic, but other types of paint would be suitable as well. The materials and tools that one uses can vary according to what is available. For example, circles can be drawn with a compass, or simply by tracing a cup, roll of tape, or other circular object. Allowing students a broad spectrum of creativity and opportunities to problem-solve within the parameters of a given project will encourage their critical thinking skills most fully.

Each project contains an italicized question somewhere in the directions. These questions are meant to be thought-provoking and promote discussion while students work on the project.

Index